Professionals in a wide range of fields have been using portfolios for years. These include artists, graphic designers, website developers, architects, marketing and communication professionals, and K-12 teachers. Think about it. How could an architect really demonstrate what she does by only telling someone what her work looked like? By using actual samples of their work, architects can give clients a much better idea of their competencies, the quality of their work, and the value they may add for an employer.

The learning and development (L&D) arena is no different. We are increasingly pressed to demonstrate what value we add to an organization. Career portfolios are becoming the passport for entry into the world of employment, or to advance in one's career. Because organizations are under pressure to hire the best employees possible, they are increasingly requiring applicants to show evidence of their expertise.

But for learning and development professionals who have never had a career portfolio, or who have used only a paper portfolio, many questions arise:

- What should be in a portfolio?

- What tools can I use to document my expertise?

- How can I be sure I'm making the best use of my portfolio?

- How do I translate my paper portfolio to an electronic format?

This TD at Work will explain what a portfolio is, how to design and develop one, how to use a portfolio in the job search, and how to use today's technology tools to assist in the process.

WHAT IS A CAREER PORTFOLIO?

A professional portfolio is a career development tool that can communicate and demonstrate an applicant's knowledge, skills, abilities, and competencies with documented evidence of performance.

A portfolio can be used in several different ways—a core one being to get a job. Not only does a career portfolio communicate your competencies, but it also provides tangible proof of your abilities in r[...] Think about a typical interview s[...] to tell what they kn[...] Wouldn't it be bett[...] samples of their wo[...] employer to assess [...]

You have undoubtedly heard that training is the first thing to be cut when budgets get tight. Portfolios provide an opportunity for learning and development professionals to demonstrate their worth to the organization using documented evidence of performance.

Just as with a resume, there is no one right way to create a career portfolio. There are no standard specifications, but there are strategies and approaches that separate good portfolios from bad ones, which we'll learn in this issue of TD at Work. A person who has a well-designed and developed portfolio will stand out when competing for jobs. In a competitive job market, if all other things are about equal, candidates without a portfolio will likely lose out to those who have one.

While portfolios are popular in many different professional fields, this TD at Work is specifically intended for professionals in the learning and development arena.

> PORTFOLIOS PROVIDE AN OPPORTUNITY FOR LEARNING AND DEVELOPMENT (L&D) PROFESSIONALS TO DEMONSTRATE THEIR WORTH TO THE ORGANIZATION USING DOCUMENTED EVIDENCE OF PERFORMANCE.

WHAT'S IN A CAREER PORTFOLIO?

There are basic elements that should be included in every portfolio, such as a bio. But portfolios are also a reflection of an individual; therefore, portfolios should be tailored to the individual career goals of each person.

Basic Portfolio Components

In addition to the work samples showcasing a worker's competencies, a portfolio includes background information about the individual. A basic career portfolio for learning and development professionals may include:

- a brief biography

- a resume, highlighting competencies and achievements

- a list of references, with names, titles, and contact information

- a client list with project descriptions

- employee evaluations or other measures of your performance

- a writing sample

- five to six examples of your work.

Additional Portfolio Components

The following items are examples of additional materials that may be included in a training professional's portfolio. The list is not meant to be inclusive.

- course design plans or evaluations

- evidence of training delivery (such as videos)

- evidence of projects you have led or managed

- training needs analysis

- multimedia productions or e-learning modules.

SELECTING ITEMS FOR YOUR PORTFOLIO

As already mentioned, it's valuable to have five to six samples of your work in your portfolio. If you have some experience in the field, ideally you will have more than five or six to choose from. To get started, gather as many good work samples as you can find to create a "master portfolio inventory" from which to choose the appropriate items. As with a resume, it is a good idea to customize your portfolio for different jobs. Think of your portfolio

as an outfit of clothing. We all have a closet that contains our clothes. If we want to work out or exercise, we select an outfit and gear for that specific task. If you are going to go to an interview, you select an appropriate outfit for that purpose. Think of your master portfolio inventory as the closet from which to choose the appropriate work samples.

For example, you may want to have one portfolio that emphasizes management of the learning function, while another may be geared for a senior instructional design position. That doesn't mean you have to create entirely new and different portfolios. You can simply choose work samples from your master portfolio inventory as appropriate. Just as you have clothing that can be worn to a number of events, you will have work samples that can be used for several different customized portfolios. See the sidebar, Questions to Ask When Selecting Portfolio Items, to guide you on which work samples to include.

> **AS WITH A RESUME, IT IS A GOOD IDEA TO CUSTOMIZE YOUR PORTFOLIO FOR DIFFERENT JOBS.**

In addition to biographical information, one item in your inventory that you can use in all of your portfolios is a writing sample. Regardless of the position's focus, all employers will be interested in your writing skills. Two types of writing samples work particularly well. One is a sample that describes your philosophy of learning or training. This type of sample not only shows potential employers how you write but also gives them some insight into your personal philosophy. Another sample could be something you've actually used in the workplace. (As I'll explain in further detail later, make sure that the sample does not contain confidential material and that you have permission to share it.) If you are applying to work in an organization that uses proposals to solicit contracts, it would be appropriate to submit a proposal that you have drafted.

In terms of selecting work samples, you should choose work that is relevant to your professional goals as well as the jobs to which you are applying.

QUESTIONS TO ASK WHEN SELECTING PORTFOLIO ITEMS

❑ Who is going to see my portfolio? Are they training professionals, or are they managers who have limited exposure to the training field?

❑ What learning and development needs does the organization have?

❑ What problems and challenges does the organization have?

❑ Which items represent my best work?

❑ Which work samples have shown positive, measurable, and impactful results?

❑ What work samples demonstrate my professional competencies?

❑ Do my work samples match up with items mentioned in the job description?

❑ How will potential employers or clients evaluate my portfolio?

❑ Does my portfolio match my resume?

And choose your best work. No one is an expert at everything. If you are not a great multimedia developer, don't dwell on that. Focus on what you can do well.

Avoid the temptation to say you have extensive instructional design experience when you don't. You can explain to the employer that you have not had an opportunity to work in that particular area, or that you have not had enough time to develop that particular skill. But let people know that you have at least basic competencies that are required for the job (only if that is true, of course).

> **REGARDLESS OF THE POSITION'S FOCUS, ALL EMPLOYERS WILL BE INTERESTED IN YOUR WRITING SKILLS.**

Let's say that you are applying for jobs that emphasize skills and competencies in instructional design. Choose items from your working portfolio that emphasize those competencies. If you are applying for a training manager position, on the other hand, select work products that emphasize your management capabilities rather than your

instructional design skills. You don't need to have a completely different portfolio for every single job, but you also don't want to have a generic portfolio that you use for every situation.

It's also important to have a well-balanced portfolio. Unless you are applying for a job as a Flash developer, your portfolio should not be filled only with examples of Flash productions that you have created.

Many people will not read your work samples all the way through. You should take this into account when you format and organize your work samples. It is appropriate to include excerpts of longer work samples, and you can use graphics and text formatting to help viewers read your work samples more easily. As always, the use of graphics and bullets, bolding, and italics will make your documents more inviting to read or view.

Finally, make sure you let employers know that you have more work samples than those you included in your portfolio. If a potential employer discusses a particular requirement at the interview that's not covered in the work samples you selected, let the interviewer know that you have experience in that area and would be happy to send a work sample that relates to that need. Providing additional work samples is a good way for you to have a reason to follow up and stay on the radar screen as a viable candidate.

It is important to note a few things. Your work samples should be aligned with your resume and cover letter. For example, your resume should mention accomplishments that are included in your portfolio, and these accomplishments should be corroborated by work samples in your portfolio. Make sure to use the same key words on both your resume and your portfolio work samples and be sure those key words are the ones included in most job announcements.

Career Goals

Without well-developed career goals, moving forward with a portfolio is a waste of time and effort—yours and, in the end, a potential employer's as well. Your career goals help you determine what to put in your portfolio. If your immediate career goal is to get a job as an instructional designer, it is pointless to have work samples that demonstrate your accounting expertise. Well-thought-out goals help guide your actions efficiently, but it takes time, effort, and some serious soul searching to develop goals. Most people find it easier to gloss over goals and dive right into their work samples. But time spent on developing your career goals will keep you focused on what you want to be doing both in the short term and long term. A beneficial resource that can help you with your search is the June 2015 *TD at Work*, "Keeping Your Career on Track."

In terms of short- and long-term goals, a helpful way of thinking is to work backward from your ultimate job. For example, if you want to become a chief learning officer or a senior project manager, what job (and skills) do you need *prior* to

SEAN'S STORY: WHEN CAN I APPLY FOR JOBS?

Is there a right time to apply for jobs? Do you have the right qualifications and experience? Are you ever ready? How do you know?

My job at the University of Maryland requires me to teach and advise adult graduate students. A lot of advising revolves around career issues.

One of my advisees with pain was Sean. He was enrolled in the master's program in instructional systems development. Sean was a special education teacher who had spent 20 years working in a K-12 public school system. He was about 40 years old and wanted to make a career transition from working with high school kids to working with adults in a teaching and learning capacity.

Sean came to me, explaining that he wanted to apply for an instructional design job he saw advertised. But he wasn't sure if he was qualified because he had completed "only" about half of his master's degree program. I assured him that he already had a lot going for him. He was an accomplished teacher and trainer, as well as a great thinker and problem solver. I saw a close enough alignment between the job ad and his skills and experience, and I encouraged Sean to apply. I told him he really had nothing to lose except the time it would take to get his application materials together.

I saw Sean a month or so later, and he was excited to report that he got the job. He told me that he was surprised because he knew that people applied who had more experience and who also already had their master's degree in instructional systems design.

After congratulating him, I asked him why he thought he got the job over the other applicants. Without hesitating, he replied that he thought his portfolio made the difference. Almost all the work samples in his portfolio were samples that he created in his graduate work at the University of Maryland. The samples demonstrated his expertise in instructional design by showcasing his design plans, instructor guides, tutorials he created using popular software authoring tools, evaluation instruments, and more. Apparently, the company was impressed with his "real world" work samples and hired him.

What are the lessons learned here? First, the power of a well-designed portfolio cannot be underestimated. Second, if your credentials are in the ballpark of what is required, then apply for the job. Finally, the only thing you have to lose when applying for jobs is time.

that job? Next, identify the job and skills you need prior to *that* job and so on.

Once you go through this process several times, it will be much easier for you to see what your career path should be and what you need to get to the next step or level.

One additional word of advice: Make sure your goals are drafted in the SMART format. That means your goals are **S**pecific, **M**easurable, **A**chievable, **R**elevant (or Results-focused), and **T**ime-bound.

Accomplishments

Where do you start when creating work samples? A good place to start is to make a list of your top career accomplishments. These can be used in your resume and your LinkedIn profile as well as in the planning of your portfolio.

What's a good accomplishment? A good accomplishment is one that solved a real problem in the workplace or improved a work situation. Additionally, a good accomplishment is measurable, for example, "Staff who took the course I created made 19 percent fewer claims processing errors." Here are some examples of job and career accomplishments:

- Created first e-learning course for the Department of Human Resources.

- Managed the design, development, and implementation of a "New Supervisor" training program.

- Reduced training vendor costs by 23 percent while maintaining the same level of service and production.

- Developed and implemented, at no cost other than staff time, the inaugural employee coaching program at the Ajax company to address employee performance.

- Created new blended employee orientation program for employees. Program enabled staff to begin their jobs faster. Received 85 percent satisfaction rating from supervisors, compared to previous rating of 53 percent.

Because I work with college students, I know how important their career is to them. But they often wonder how to create a portfolio when they are first entering the professional world. At this point, your accomplishments may be projects you've completed for school or through volunteer opportunities. Many associations seek professional assistance pro bono. And if you have completed an internship, experience gained through it is another possibility. See the sidebar, How Can I Get Experience? for additional advice.

ORGANIZING YOUR PORTFOLIO

As I mentioned early in this issue of *TD at Work*, just as there are many ways to organize a resume, there are many ways to organize your portfolio; the following model is one. No matter which organizational model you opt for, you should keep in mind a few guiding questions:

- Who will be reading it?

- Will readers be knowledgeable about the content?

- Have you chosen your best and most appropriate work?

- What do the readers know about the L&D profession?

- Will you always have a chance to present your portfolio, or will it be open to interpretation?

Your portfolio should be organized and easy to navigate. You should have work samples labeled and have an introductory cover sheet for each. Put yourself in the shoes of the viewers or the readers. How will they want to see information laid out? What type of navigation would they like to see or use? What information needs to be labeled?

A good practice is to have someone from outside your field read your portfolio. Having a pair of fresh eyes—especially those of someone not familiar with the acronyms and nomenclature of a particular profession—can provide you with valuable feedback on how to organize your information. The last thing you want is for readers to not be able to find or understand the information that they view.

Because today's portfolios are often digital, most work samples will be an electronic file of

HOW CAN I GET EXPERIENCE?

A big dilemma for job seekers is having the required experience to get hired. How do people get experience if they don't have it? Another question revolves around career changers who have little experience in a new field: What can they do? How can you develop work samples without experience?

The good news is that you do have options. The bad news is that there are no quick fixes. Getting experience will take some time, and you need to be patient.

There are many organizations out there in need of help that may be able to give you the opportunity to build experience. The three most promising options are:

- professional associations

- nonprofit organizations

- schools.

Professional Associations

If you are interested in getting into the field of learning and development or instructional design, one way to make contacts and identify opportunities is to join a professional association such as the Association for Talent Development (ATD), the e-Learning Guild, or other similar organization. If you are a student, many professional associations have heavily discounted student memberships such as the one ATD provides for students (www.td.org/Members/Student-Membership).

Professional associations usually have local chapters that hold regional meetings, giving you ready access to a local network in the field. By attending local chapter meetings, you can learn about the latest trends while building a network of professional colleagues.

Most local chapters need volunteers to help organize meetings, identify speakers, market programs, and manage their chapter websites. Volunteering to help run your local chapter can provide excellent opportunities to build skills, experience, and relationships.

Nonprofit Organizations

Nonprofit organizations are always in need of expertise and are often short of funds. If you are not a student, nonprofits are one of your best sources for volunteer work because for-profits are restricted to offering unpaid internships to students.

If you're not sure where to begin, look at the opportunities on a site like Volunteer Match (www.volunteermatch.org); Idealist (www.idealist.org); the Taproot Foundation (www.taprootfoundation.org); or a local volunteer sourcing organization (most cities have a list of volunteer opportunities).

If none of the listed opportunities meet your needs, identify some local nonprofit organizations you'd like to work with and contact them. If you have no idea whom to contact, I recommend searching the organization's website or LinkedIn profile. Usually, a good place to start is human resources or the education or volunteer coordinator. Research the organization online to identify some areas of need for the organization that you can help with. For example, if you know you need to develop some work samples in e-learning, identify organizations that need to provide education in your community. Almost all nonprofit and community organizations do this sort of outreach, so you should be able to find many opportunities to build your skills.

Talk to your contacts about being an unpaid intern or a volunteer. Tell them that you want to work on projects that will help build out your professional portfolio. There are many organizations out there that would love to have help, so don't settle for projects that do not help you build your professional skills. In theory, you can work as many or as few hours as you would like, although some organizations will require specific commitments. In a rare instance where things don't work out, you are free to move on to another organization that is more compatible with your interests.

HOW CAN I GET EXPERIENCE? (CONTINUED)

Schools

If you are a full-time student, your options for gaining experience and building your portfolio are more numerous. Class work, paid and unpaid internships, and extracurricular activities all provide opportunities to build your skills. Review current job ads for the type of position that you wish to find and identify the skills that are most frequently requested. This will help you to focus your efforts on the areas that matter most to employers.

Paid Opportunities

It is sometimes possible to gain experience with a for-profit organization through contract work, part-time opportunities, or organized paid internships. Sites such as Internships.com and Flexjobs.com may provide you with some leads. And members of the local chapter of your professional association may be able to assist you with ideas and leads.

While it can be more difficult to find paid opportunities to gain experience, if your skills are in demand, you may be able to apply for a position on the strength of the work samples you developed in school or through a certificate program (see the sidebar, Sean's Story).

So, while it will take some extra effort on your part, gaining experience in a new field is possible if you are both patient and creative!

---

some sort. The file should have a descriptive file name (such as yourname_design_plan.pdf or your name_job_aid2.pdf). The cover sheet that introduces the work sample should list the competency the work sample demonstrates (competency); provide a context (context); describe what the applicant did (action); and describe the outcomes (results).

The easiest way to do this is to use the following simple C-CAR format.

C ompetency:	Identify the competency.
C ontext:	Describe the situation.
A ction:	Describe what you did and why.
R esults:	Describe outcomes, using measurable results if possible.

Here are some example introductions using the C-CAR format.

Example 1

C ompetency:	Learning design.
C ontext:	Sales revenue down after hiring new sales reps.
A ction:	Created company's first online sales training course.
R esults:	Sales revenue rose 24.7 percent a quarter after the course was implemented.

Example 2

C ompetency:	Training delivery.
C ontext:	Remote staff can't get training. New employees made 27 percent more errors processing claims.
A ction:	Taught company's first online course in claims processing.
R esults:	Claims processing errors reduced by 17 percent after the course was implemented.

In terms of the C-CAR format, the good news is that we work in an industry where the competencies and standards are already well defined. The competencies that may be the most familiar are those established by the Association for Talent Development (ATD). See the sidebar, ATD Competency Model, for details.

ATD is the premier professional association in our field, but there are other associations that have learning and development competency models. The first is the International Society of Performance Improvement (ISPI); more information can be found at www.ispi.org. A second is the International Board of Standards for Training, Performance, and Instruction (IBSTPI), which can be found at http://ibstpi.org. These organizations have a slightly different approach and philosophy, which may be helpful to review.

You may be unsure about identifying your competencies. Organizations increasingly value a potential employee who shows the ability to achieve results like these:

- increased revenue or resources

- increased efficiency

- decreased staff time

- decreased costs.

It may be helpful to keep these competencies in mind when you create and polish your work samples.

It is your responsibility to educate others about yourself and your skills. Using the C-CAR format is an excellent way to explain who you are, what you have accomplished, and how it helped the organization.

CAREER PORTFOLIO TOOLS

In the past, portfolios were created and shared in hard-copy format and given in person to prospective employers. Today we often create and share portfolios digitally using websites or file-sharing programs such as Google Drive or Dropbox. Using these programs helps you control who has access to your files.

Many hiring managers don't care if work samples are posted on a website. Unless you are applying to be a website developer, the website is merely the wrapper in which a work sample is

ATD COMPETENCY MODEL

The following are talent development competencies as listed by the Association for Talent Development (ATD) in its 2014 Competency Model:

- *Performance Improvement.* Apply a systematic process for analyzing human performance gaps and for closing them.

- *Instructional Design.* Design and develop informal and formal learning solutions using a variety of methods.

- *Training Delivery.* Deliver informal and formal learning solutions in a manner that is both engaging and effective.

- *Learning Technologies.* Apply a variety of learning technologies to address specific learning needs.

- *Evaluating Learning Impact.* Use learning metrics and analytics to measure the impact of learning solutions.

- *Managing Learning Programs.* Provide leadership to execute the organization's people strategy; implement training projects and activities.

- *Integrated Talent Management.* Build an organization's culture, capability, capacity, and engagement through people development strategies.

- *Coaching.* Apply a systematic process to improve others' ability to set goals, take action, and maximize strengths.

- *Knowledge Management.* Capture, distribute, and archive intellectual capital to encourage knowledge sharing and collaboration.

- *Change Management.* Apply a systematic process to shift individuals, teams, and organizations from current state to desired state.

More detailed competency information can be found on the ATD website at www.td.org/Certification/Competency-Model.

contained. The most important thing is the work sample itself. Therefore, making work samples available using file-sharing programs is usually sufficient.

Creating an Electronic Portfolio

While creating an electronic portfolio can be daunting, it's actually much simpler than it used to be. Most portfolios can be created using simple files and links to hosted content such as videos or multimedia productions (using, for example, Adobe Captivate or Articulate Storyline). The idea is to create your work samples in a format that can be easily displayed, shared, and distributed electronically.

There are three or four basic types of files used for work samples.

Text Documents: Text documents can be shared as PDFs or Microsoft Word files. PDF files, as opposed to files created with Microsoft Word, may be preferred because they are widely used and the Adobe Acrobat reader software is free. PDF files cannot be edited and are more likely to display properly because they are essentially pictures of your document.

Videos: Video files are the next type of file that is commonly used in portfolios. The most common types are WMV, MPEG-4, and MOV file formats. Posting your videos to YouTube is likely your best bet. Nearly all people know how to play video that is posted on a YouTube site.

Proprietary Formats: Another common type of file used in portfolios are those created with Adobe Captivate, Articulate Storyline, or similar authoring tools. Avoid offering work samples in obscure or proprietary file formats that the average person may not be able to open. As with asking someone else to read your portfolio, it also makes sense to get someone who is not in our field to "test drive" your work samples.

Using a Website for Your Portfolio

You can now create your own website without having any in-depth technical knowledge. There are a number of free and low-cost website creation tools that work quite well. These tools provide templates that you can customize to fit your own needs.

If you decide to create your own website or use one that someone has created for you, the site needs to be simple, uncluttered, and easy to navigate and use. But note: Having a website is not required! Your time is better spent on improving your work samples.

Some of the more popular free or low-cost website development tools are:

- WordPress.com, a very popular platform that allows users to create their website for free. It has several different plug-ins and templates.

- Google's iSite and other Google sites that function like blogs and include widgets and integration with many other Google tools.

- Weebly, an easy-to-use platform that also provides free access to a collection of images for noncopyrighted use.

- Wix, which uses drag-and-drop widgets to give you flexibility in placement of items.

- Joomla.com, similar to WordPress, has predesigned templates.

- Adobe Muse, a build-your-own platform that requires no programming skills or knowledge.

These are just a few of the more common tools; there are many others. Because technology is dynamic, new products are being developed all the time. Worth noting is Behance.net, which supports many file-sharing types that the other tools do not, including interactive programs, which may make it a better tool to showcase creative portfolios.

The University of Wisconsin-Stout has posted a rubric for assessing—either by yourself or by asking others to do so—how user-friendly your e-portfolio is, whether it has grammatical errors, and the like (see References and Resources).

The biggest caution with website development is the time it requires. While you may not need in-depth technical expertise to create a website, it will take time. It is more important to spend time creating and polishing your work samples than it is to have a website.

Another thing that can take up a significant amount of time is the maintenance of your website. Posting files, changing website navigation, and updating software is time-consuming. The site also needs to be backed up, and you need to decide what you will do if your site goes down. If you decide to create a website, be sure to have a plan in place to handle these issues.

> IF YOU DECIDE TO CREATE YOUR OWN WEBSITE OR USE ONE THAT SOMEONE HAS CREATED FOR YOU, THE SITE NEEDS TO BE SIMPLE, UNCLUTTERED, AND EASY TO NAVIGATE AND USE.

Using File-Sharing Programs for Your Portfolio

Websites are not the only way to distribute your portfolio. The fastest and easiest way to share your work samples may be by using file-sharing programs.

These are some of the more common free programs for sharing and distributing your work samples:

- Box

- Dropbox

- Google Drive.

In general, these programs are easy to use. Because many people already use these popular programs, there may be no learning curve for the recipients of your work samples.

These programs have individual differences, but they provide many of the same features, including:

- syncing with other devices (for example, iPad and tablets, iPhone, Android)

- control over who has access

- easy ways to share content to email, Facebook, Twitter, and other social media

- ability to access anywhere

- storage backup.

The remote access feature may be useful during interviews if you need to share work samples on the spot.

Note that additional costs may be incurred for increased storage capabilities and premium features.

Incorporating Video Into Your Portfolio

Video has become a critical tool in the trainer's toolkit, and I strongly encourage you to include it in your work samples. Depending on the role you seek, you may include a video of yourself teaching or training. Another idea is to have a short video (less than two minutes) that tells prospective employers who you are and what you have to offer their organization.

Such videos can make quite an impression on employers and make you stand out from the crowd. They can be akin to the "elevator speech" and also can relay your training philosophy. Most people would rather watch a video than read text in a document or on a website. Including a video not only makes your portfolio more appealing for users, it also illustrates your technology skills.

In the past, creating, editing, and publishing video was expensive and difficult. Today, with affordable cameras, such as home camcorders and smartphones, it is pretty easy to capture high-quality video. Additionally, the editing process has become much more simple and affordable. With free and low-cost editing software—such as Windows Movie Maker, Adobe Premiere Elements, Apple iMovie, and Lightworks—there is no reason someone cannot create a simple video.

Technology Work Samples

Learning technology is an important competency. If you look at job advertisements in the L&D field, you will notice that many jobs require technology skills. The following are possible work samples related to learning technology competencies:

- products you created using authoring tools

- video created using Apple's iMovie and Microsoft's Movie Maker

- audio podcasts or instructional audio created using software such as Audacity

- screen tours created using Captivate or Camtasia

SOFTWARE TOOLS TO CREATE, PUBLISH, AND SHARE PORTFOLIOS

These are some of the software and learning tools learning and development professionals commonly use to create and share their portfolios electronically.

Audacity
Audacity is a free, easy-to-use audio editor and recorder for Windows, Mac OS X, GNU/Linux, and other operating systems. In addition to recording, it can cut, copy, splice, and mix sounds together.

Box and Dropbox
Box and Dropbox are free file-sharing tools. You can use them to store, manage, and share your files securely in the cloud and access your content anywhere you might need it via the web, tablet, or smartphone. You also can share large files with a simple link from any device. This is a quick and easy way to share the work samples in your portfolio.

Camtasia
Camtasia Studio is a screen video capture program for Microsoft Windows. It can record your screen and create, for example, training videos or other multimedia productions.

iMovie
iMovie is a video-editing software application that allows Mac users to edit their own home movies. It was originally released by Apple in 1999. iMovie imports video footage into a computer where the user can then edit the video clips and add titles and music. Effects include basic color correction and video enhancement tools and transitions such as fade-in, fade-out, and slides.

Keynote
Keynote is a presentation software application developed as a part of Apple's iWork productivity suite (which also includes Pages and Numbers). It is Apple's version of Microsoft's PowerPoint.

Snagit
Snagit allows users to capture graphics or enhance images. It also is a screencasting program that can record audio and anything that appears on your PC screen and save it as a video. It is a powerful tool with an easy-to-use interface that contains features needed by technical writers (for example, scrolling page screenshots and automatic "trim edges" function).

Emerging Software Tools
Because new tools are constantly emerging, you need to keep abreast of changes. One way to do this is by visiting the "Top 100 Learning Tools" at the Centre for Learning and Performance Technologies at http://c4lpt.co.uk/directory/top-100-tools.

- online surveys created using Zoomerang or Survey Monkey
- samples of your multimedia production for learning
- job aids you designed and developed using instructional technology
- websites you created
- narrated PowerPoint (or other multimedia) learning modules you created.

SHARING YOUR PORTFOLIO

One of the main reasons to have a portfolio is to convince prospective employers that you have the knowledge, skills, and competencies you need to get a job. Many jobs are now filled by recruiters who contact people who are not actively looking for a new job. This changes the whole job search dynamic. To portray yourself in the best light and to learn about new opportunities that could propel your career, you need to proactively share information about your expertise.

One of the easiest ways to do this is to use social media. While social media may still have a bad reputation with some people—for example, because of privacy or security concerns—it is difficult to deny its reach and power in the professional realm. See the sidebar, Managing Your Online Content, for guidance on creating an appropriate online presence.

Today's social media simply is a marketing and communication tool to help you get noticed as a subject matter expert. The key is to use the right type of social media for your purposes. For example, you can provide feedback and comments on blogs, professional Facebook pages, Twitter, and more.

Once people see that you know what you are talking about, they will want to learn more and will often check out your profile and work samples. Many consultants use this technique to get established and keep their name active. It can be a lucrative way to get consulting contracts, speaking engagements, and other professional opportunities.

MANAGING YOUR ONLINE CONTENT

Sometimes getting the job is contingent upon making a great first impression, and that first impression may be what is found online. If you choose to post your career information or your portfolio online, people can and will make judgments about you.

Recruiters are using social media at an ever-increasing level to check out prospective candidates. If what they see reflects negatively on you, you may never even get an interview. However, if they see complimentary postings from professional colleagues and well-designed work samples, it will enhance your professional reputation.

First, a few don'ts. Don't post your work phone number or your work email. Never post your home address; however, if you want employers to know that you are local, you can include your city or town of residence.

Now some dos. Ideally you want to give potential employers a taste of what you can do professionally. Do post some "teaser" work samples that pique viewers' interest. Let them know that you have more to share. Consider posting your resume in a functional format with accomplishments listed by competency or category. Although recruiters tend to dislike this type of resume from job applicants, in your online portfolio it can serve as a brochure that shows the types of services you have to offer an employer.

If you use social media or have worked in an online environment, you are probably aware of the privacy issues associated with the digital world. Controlling your personal and professional information is important, and it isn't always easy to stay on top of everything. You may have created, posted, and forgotten your resume and other types of career information on different accounts. You may have a Facebook site that combines personal and professional information. If you are applying for jobs or seeking consulting opportunities, take some time to review all of your online profiles to make sure that they are up-to-date. Remove or delete anything that is out-of-date or inconsistent with the online presence you wish to share with the world. It can be difficult to completely remove items from the web once they are posted, but with diligence you should be able to remove the offending items.

According to Minda Zetlin's *Inc.* article, "Why You Should Google Yourself Regularly (and What to Do About What You Find)," it is a good practice to Google your own name occasionally to see what shows up. You may be surprised what you find. If so, you may need to take action to correct it.

Social media is a very powerful tool for marketing and promoting yourself. However, you need to review your content periodically, using the above guidelines, to make sure you are creating a great first impression.

LinkedIn is the most popular career-related social media platform. It has nearly 400 million users around the world. Because users can search for people and jobs by using key words, LinkedIn has become a favorite tool of recruiters. According to Jobvite's 2015 Recruiter Nation study, 92 percent of recruiters use social media, and of those, 87 percent use LinkedIn—well above the 55 percent who use Facebook. As a result, not having an account means that recruiters and employers are far less likely to find you. While you may not get any points for being on LinkedIn, you probably lose some points by not having a professional profile on the site.

LinkedIn also has more than 2 million groups that members can join to share professional and career-related information. In addition to the Association for Talent Development group on LinkedIn, you may want to consider the eLearning Industry, Organization Development and Training, and the Workplace Learning and Performance Forum.

Another advantage to LinkedIn is that you can share your resume or work samples on your profile. For example, you may want to post documents and presentations, links to videos that are hosted elsewhere, and links to presentations in SlideShare.

> **WHILE YOU MAY NOT GET ANY POINTS FOR BEING ON LINKEDIN, YOU PROBABLY LOSE SOME POINTS BY NOT HAVING A PROFESSIONAL PROFILE ON THE SITE.**

Items can be added, edited, moved, or removed from your LinkedIn profile from the *Edit Profile* page. As with all technology, things are changing quickly, so check LinkedIn for the latest instructions.

As mentioned in the Jobvite study, Facebook is also popular and is increasingly being used by recruiters in addition to LinkedIn. Be cautious about mixing your personal and professional information on one Facebook page.

Instead, consider creating a separate "page" with a unique website address under your original (personal) account. This way, you can post all your professional items and thoughts on one page and keep your personal Facebook posts and birthday party pictures separate. I have two Facebook pages under one account: My personal Facebook page is www.facebook.com/gregwilliams123, but my professional Facebook page is www.facebook.com/elearningforeverybody.

Many times, applicants are required to submit an electronic application and resume to prospective employers. It is imperative that you list an active link to your portfolio on your resume. You want employers to view your portfolio, so make it easy for them to do so.

USING YOUR PORTFOLIO

Up until this point, we've mainly been discussing how to use your portfolio in the job search process. Here are a few more ways to use your portfolio:

Interviews

Most interviews are fairly predictable. For example, one of the typical questions is "What are your greatest accomplishments?" This is the perfect opportunity for you to talk about your accomplishments and show work samples that demonstrate your achievements.

Essentially, your potential employer or client wants to understand your strengths and weaknesses, why they should hire you, and how you are different from other candidates. Your answers to these questions should be rehearsed until your responses sound natural. A common mistake people make when it comes to interviews is that they don't practice beforehand. Interviewing is a skill and skills improve with practice.

Ideally, each answer you give should be backed up with a specific work sample in your portfolio that proves you have the skills you claim to possess. Showing your work provides powerful evidence that you have the ability to do what you claim. However, be careful about sharing your work samples without first asking interviewers if they would like to view them during the interview. They might prefer to look at your portfolio after

YOUR PORTFOLIO AND PROPRIETARY INFORMATION

Many jobs involve information that may be considered secret, confidential, or proprietary, or that may provide a competitive advantage. Information like this may be found at private companies, military organizations, or organizations that simply don't want certain information to be public. As you can understand, situations such as this may be an issue for learning and development professionals. We may have some great work samples that we cannot share beyond our own company.

So what can you do? First, you need to find out the company policy about sharing information outside of the organization; some organizations have strict policies about not doing so. Other organizations may limit what you share.

Second, if your organization allows you to display certain information, here are some things to consider:

- Choose work samples that do not include information that meets the commonsense questionable threshold, for example, employee orientation and safety information.

- Edit information. You may redact, white out, or change organization names. Instead of naming your company, for example, you can just say a "midsize manufacturing organization" or the "Acme Company" or another fictitious name. It is also possible to take excerpts of work samples. Say you have a 50-page design plan. Because most prospective employers will not need to review every page of your work plan, you can provide 10 to 15 pages that do not share any objectionable or questionable information.

Whatever you do, make sure that your employer agrees before you display or publicly share any information. If your employer does not allow you to share any information, you may need to consider working as a volunteer. You can do this with another organization that does permit information to be shared (see sidebar, How Can I Get Experience?).

the interview, so be sure that you have a leave-behind that will enable them to do so.

Performance Appraisals

Performance appraisals and employee evaluations also provide opportunities to use your portfolio. Ideally, you have not had the experience of having a boss who cannot remember what you have achieved during the year. Unfortunately, this happens more often than most people realize. By using work samples in this process, employees can make it easy for their supervisor to remember what they have accomplished.

Like an interview, performance appraisals are usually predictable. Employees typically have individual goals that the employee and supervisor have agreed on. If the goals are drafted well, it should be relatively simple to prove that the goals have been met (the goals should be SMART, just like your career goals that you developed at the beginning of the process).

It is helpful to have a one-page statement that provides your supervisor with the summary of your accomplishments and achievements. These items should be linked to specific work samples. The goal is to make it easy for your supervisor to see what you did and how it made a difference in your organization.

> **BE CAREFUL ABOUT SHARING YOUR WORK SAMPLES WITHOUT FIRST ASKING INTERVIEWERS IF THEY WOULD LIKE TO VIEW THEM DURING THE INTERVIEW.**

Your Professional Development

The purpose of a career portfolio is to provide evidence of your professional performance. Work samples can be very personal, and people are often uncomfortable sharing their work outside their own work environment. However, to improve, we need feedback on our performance. Seek out qualified people to give you meaningful input on your work samples. Then, use this advice to improve your portfolio.

Networking and Marketing Yourself

If you are active in social media and on professional blogs, people are more likely to review your professional profile. Portfolios can be a useful tool to market yourself and make networking connections. As previously mentioned, having a well-thought-out LinkedIn profile is one of the easiest ways to establish an online presence. Because your profile is public, only post items that you feel comfortable displaying for all to see. Be careful not to share any items that include proprietary or confidential information, or material that your employer may not want to make public.

Many consultants use LinkedIn to establish themselves as subject matter experts. They post samples of the work that they have completed for satisfied clients. If you were looking for a building contractor to remodel your kitchen, it would be nice to see samples of their work. The same applies in this situation. But again, make sure the information is not something the client is unwilling to share; it's good to ask for their OK to post.

CONCLUSION

So what does the future hold for portfolios?

Learning and development is one of the professions that will see a significant increase in the use of portfolios. The use of technology to create and display portfolios will undoubtedly increase.

In the future, it will be commonplace for trainers to have videos of themselves teaching a class or multimedia tutorials that they created posted online. And in many cases, the future jobs in the L&D field will require more applicants to submit portfolios electronically. There will also be a greater push to have portfolio content that can be accessed or viewed through mobile devices such as smartphones.

As you've seen from Sean's story, career portfolios are one way that you can differentiate yourself from other job applicants. Career portfolios may soon be as common in this field as they are for other architects, artists, and graphic designers.

Tomorrow they may be a requirement; today, they are a tool that can give you a leg up. Use it to your advantage and prepare for the future.

Books

Bolles, R. N. 2014. *What Color Is Your Parachute? 2015: A Practical Manual for Job-Hunters and Career-Changers.* Danvers, MA: Ten Speed Press.

Articles

Hayman, A. 2009. "How to Develop an Instructional Design ePortfolio–Part 3." Z(e)n Learning, August 3. https://aprilhayman.wordpress.com/2009/08/03/isdeportfoliopart3.

Lankford, L.A. 2011. "ISD Professionals: Building a Portfolio." Training Pros: Leighanne's Learning Notes, February 14. https://ileighanne.wordpress.com/2011/02/14/isd-professionals-building-a-portfolio.

Malamed, C. n.d. "Answers to Instructional Design Career Questions." The eLearning Coach. http://theelearningcoach.com/elearning_design/isd/instructional-design-career-questions.

Singer, M. 2015. "Welcome to the 2015 Recruiter Nation, Formerly Known as the Social Recruiting Survey." Jobvite, September 22. www.jobvite.com/blog/welcome-to-the-2015-recruiter-nation-formerly-known-as-the-social-recruiting-survey.

Williams, G. 2012. "Using a Career Portfolio." Career Development Blog, October 17. www.td.org/Publications/Blogs/Career-Development-Blog/2012/10/Using-a-Career-Portfolio.

Zetlin, M. 2015. "Why You Should Google Yourself Regularly (and What to Do About What You Find)." *Inc.*, November 18. www.inc.com/minda-zetlin/why-you-should-google-yourself-regularly-and-what-to-do-about-what-you-find-inf.html.

Websites

Centre for Learning and Performance Technologies (C4LPT) by Jane Hart: http://c4lpt.co.uk/directory/top-100-tools.

Creating ePortfolios with Web 2.0 Tools by Helen Barrett: http://electronicportfolios.org/web20portfolios.html.

Developing an ePortfolio by the Instructional Design Career Center at the University of Wisconsin-Stout: www2.uwstout.edu/content/profdev/idjobsearch/portfolio.html.

Free Technology for Teachers by Richard Byrne: www.freetech4teachers.com.

Idealist: www.idealist.org.

The Taproot Foundation: www.taprootfoundation.org.

Volunteer Match: www.volunteermatch.org.

FORMATTING WORK SAMPLES FOR YOUR PORTFOLIO

Directions: Select one of your work samples and organize it into the C-CAR format using the categories below. See the example for guidance.

C ompetency: Identify the competency.

C ontext :   Describe the situation.

A ction: Describe what you did and why.

R esults: Describe outcomes, using measurable results if possible.

C-CAR Format Example

C ompetency: Learning Design
C ontext: Sales revenue down after hiring new sales reps.
A ction: Created company's first online sales training course.
R esults: Sales revenue rose 24.7 percent a quarter after the course was implemented.

REQUIRED SKILLS VS. MY EXPERIENCE

This is a simple table to help you determine whether you have the experience for a particular job. You can use this for any job, not just an instructional design or training job. Look at the job description and cut and paste the required skills and experience into the left column. Then, in the right column, fill in your own skills and experience that address these requirements. Remember that your skills and experience should be corroborated by your work samples.

Some examples are below.

Skills and Experience Required in Ad	My Skills and Experience

Example 1: Instructional Designer

Skills and Experience Required in Ad	My Skills and Experience
Minimum of three (3) years of professional experience designing, developing, and managing online, blended, or other technology-mediated instruction.	I have 4.5 years of experience designing and developing face-to-face and online instruction. See work samples 3 and 4 in my portfolio for the Captivate modules I created for online learning.
Collaborate and consult with subject matter experts and communication specialists to design, develop, and deliver online, face-to-face, and blended learning experiences.	I have created 18 course modules by collaborating with SMEs. See work samples 5 and 6 in my portfolio as examples.
Familiarity with graphic design principles appropriate for developing online, face-to-face, and blended instruction, as well as print-based learning materials, is required.	Created all the graphic design elements for three years in my first job for both online and blended course materials. See work samples 1 and 2 in my portfolio.

Example 2: Training Manager

Skills and Experience Required in Ad	My Skills and Experience
Manage production and coordination, and oversee revisions of curriculum for online courses.	I served as project manager for four years where I was responsible for supervising instructional designers and e-learning development staff to produce 27 online courses. See work samples 1 and 2 in my portfolio.
Facilitate production, coordination, and updates for train-the-trainer programs to include creation of curriculums, facilitator manuals, and participant guides.	I have created both instructor and participant manuals for two separate Train the Trainer courses. See work samples 3 and 4 in my portfolio.
Oversee faculty vetting and development through in-service program.	I have hired and vetted nearly two dozen trainers in a four-year period. Ninety-seven percent of the trainers I hired received a good or excellent rating by employees.